GW00319253

At a pub in Crosby, a newcomer ask
here all your life?"

After a long pause the man replied "Don't know yet!"

A man made a phone call and asked "What time does the library open?"

"Nine am" came the reply. "And what's the idea of calling me at home in the middle of the night to ask a question like that?"

"Not until nine am?" the man asked in a disappointed voice. "No, not till nine am!" the librarian replied. "Why do you want to get in before nine am?"

"Who said I wanted to get in?" the man sighed sadly. "I want to get out."

A couple from St Helens both retired at the same time. The husband had always had a dream about being able to play the piano, so his wife bought him a piano for his birthday. A few weeks later, her friend asked how he was getting on with it. "Oh, we returned the piano." said the other woman, "I persuaded him to switch to the oboe instead."

"Why's that?" asked her friend "Because," she answered, "with an oboe, he can't sing."

LIVERPOOL
Wit & Humour

MERCY POOLE

BRADWELL
BOOKS

Published by Bradwell Books

9 Orgreave Close Sheffield S13 9NP

Email: books@bradwellbooks.co.uk

Compiled by Mercy Poole

British Library Cataloguing in Publication Data: a catalogue record for
this book is available from the British Library.

1st Edition

ISBN: 9781909914438

Print: Gomer Press, Llandysul, Ceredigion SA44 4JL

Design by: jenksdesign@yahoo.co.uk/07506 471162

Illustrations: ©Tim O'Brien 2014

Three Liverpool fans and three Manchester United fans were going on day trip by train. At the train station, the three United fans each bought their tickets and watched in confusion as the three Scousers bought just one ticket between them. "How are three people going to travel on only one ticket?" asked one of the Manchester United group. "Watch this!" answered one of the Liverpool group.

The fans got onto the train. But while the Man United fans sat in their seats, all three of the Scousers crowded into the train toilet and closed the door behind them.

Shortly after the train left, the conductor came round to check tickets. He knocked on the toilet door and said, "Ticket, please!" The door opened a fraction and a single arm emerged with a ticket in hand. The conductor took it, checked it and moved on. The United fans watched all this and agreed it was quite a clever idea. So, on the return trip, they decided to copy the Liverpool fans on the return trip and save some money. When they got to the station, they bought a single ticket for the return trip. To their astonishment, the Liverpool fans didn't buy a ticket at all. "How are you going to travel without a ticket?" asks one perplexed United follower. "Watch" said one of the Scousers.

When they got onto the train, the three Man United fans all crammed together into a toilet and the three Liverpool supporters squished into another one nearby. The train started up. Shortly afterwards, one of the Liverpool group left the toilet and walked over to the toilet in which the United fans were hiding. He knocked on the door and said, "Ticket, please."

One day, a Liverpool fan arrived at Anfield for a big match. He was a little late and the match soon kicked off. The fan was surprised to notice that the seat next to him was still empty. He asked the man on the other side of the empty seat if the person was with him.

"No." answered the man, "It's my wife's seat, but she died suddenly."

"Oh I'm so sorry, mate," said the other man "...couldn't you have given it to a friend or relative or something?"

"I would have done" said the other man, "But they've all gone to the funeral."

Two blokes from Sefton went into a pub.

The first man said "A pint o' bitter, and a half o' shandy for my mate 'Donkey', please!"

The publican replied "What's with him calling you 'Donkey'?"

The second one said "Oh, 'e aw, 'e aw, 'e always calls me that!"

What did the centipede sing to his girlfriend? I Wanna Hold Your Hand Hand Hand Hand Hand....

A farmer from down south once visited a farmer in Prescot. The first farmer asked "How big is your farm?" to which the farmer replied "Can you see those trees over there? That's the boundary of my farmland"

The farmer responded, "Wow. It takes me three days to drive to the boundary of my farm."

The man said "I had a car like that once."

A rather cocky man working on a busy construction site in Bootle was bragging that he could outdo anyone in a feat of strength. He made a special case of making fun of Morris, one of the more senior workmen. After several minutes, Morris had had enough.

"Why don't you put your money where your mouth is?" he said. "I'll bet a week's wages that I can haul something in a wheelbarrow over to that outbuilding that you won't be able to wheel back."

"You're on, mate," the over confident young man replied. "It's a bet! Let's see what you got."

Morris reached out and grabbed the wheelbarrow by the handles. Then, nodding to the young man, he said, "All right. Get in."

A man from Earlestown was staggering home one evening, after a heavy night at the pub with his friends.

He suddenly noticed a man from the water board with a big 'T' handle, in the middle of the road opening a valve at the bottom of a manhole.

He walked up behind him and gave him a shove.

"What was that for?" asked the startled man.

The drunken man replied, "That's for turning all the streets round when I'm trying to find my way home!"

A life-long city man, tired of the rat race in his home town of London, decided he was going to give up the city life, move to the Wirral, and become a chicken farmer. He bought a chicken farm Heswall and moved in. It turned out that his next door neighbour was also a chicken farmer. The neighbour came for a visit one day and said, "Chicken farming isn't easy. I know. To help you get started, I'll give you 100 chickens."

The new chicken farmer was delighted. Two weeks later the neighbour dropped by to see how things were going. The new farmer said, "Not too well mate. All 100 chickens died." The neighbour said, "Oh, I can't believe that. I've never had any trouble with my chickens. I'll give you 100 more." Another two weeks went by and the neighbour dropped in again. The new farmer said, "You're not going to believe this, but the second

100 chickens died too." Astounded, the neighbour asked, "What went wrong?"

The new farmer said, "Well, I'm not sure whether I'm planting them too deep or too close together."

Have you heard about the latest machine at the amusement arcade in Kirkdale?

You put ten pence in and ask it any question and it gives you a true answer.

One holiday maker from Liverpool tried it last week.

He asked the machine "Where is my father?" The machine replied:

"Your father is fishing in Wales."

Well, he thought, that's daft for a start because my father is dead.

"Where is my mother's husband?"

Back came the reply, "Your mother's husband is buried in Prescot, but your father is still fishing in Wales."

What did George Harrison say to his guitar while it gently weeped

Don't Fret.

Did you hear about the truck driver from Fazakerly who was seen desperately chiselling away at the brickwork after his lorry got stuck while passing through a tunnel?

"Why don't you let some air out of your tyres?" asked a helpful passer-by.

"No, mate," replied the driver "It's the roof that won't go under, not the wheels."

BEWARE LOW BRIDGE!

It was a quiet night in Everton and a man and his wife were tucked up in bed fast asleep when there was an unexpected knock on the door. The man looked at his clock and saw that it was half past three in the morning. "I'm not getting out of bed at this time of the night," he thought, and rolled over.

A louder knock followed. "Aren't you going to answer that?" asked his wife sleepily.

So the man dragged himself out of bed and went downstairs. He opened the door and saw that there was a strange man standing at the door. It didn't take the homeowner long to realise that the man was drunk.

"Hi there," slurred the stranger. "Can you give me a push?"

"No, I'm sorry. It's half past three. I was in bed," said the man and slammed the door. He went back up to bed and told his wife what happened.

"That wasn't very nice of you," she said.

"Remember that night we broke down in the pouring rain on the way to pick the kids up from the babysitter, and you had to knock on that man's door to get us started again? What would have happened if he'd told us to get lost?"

"But the man who just knocked on our door was drunk," replied her husband.

"Well we can at least help move his car somewhere safe and sort him out a taxi," said his wife. "He needs our help." So the husband got out of bed again, got dressed, and went downstairs. He opened the door, but couldn't to see the stranger anywhere so he shouted, "Hey, do you still want a push?" In answer, he heard a voice call out, "Yes please!" So, still being unable to see the stranger, he shouted,

"Where are you?"

"I'm over here," the stranger replied, "on your swing."

Pete and Larry hadn't seen each other in many years. They were having a long chat, telling each other all about their lives. Finally Pete invited Larry to visit him in his new apartment in Liverpool city centre. "I have a wife and three kids and I'd love to have you visit us."

"Great. Where do you live?"

"Here's the address. There's plenty of parking behind the flat. Park and come around to the front door, kick it open with your foot, go to the lift and press the button with your left elbow, then enter! When you reach the sixth floor, go down the hall until you see my name on the door. Then press the doorbell with your right elbow and I'll let you in."

"Great. But tell me...what is all this business of kicking the front door open, then pressing lift buttons with my right, then my left elbow?"

Pete answered, "Surely you're not coming empty-handed?".

Which Beatles song is about their favourite vegetable? Peas Please Me!

Two boys were arguing when the teacher entered the room.

The teacher asked, "Why are you arguing?"

One boy answered, "We found a ten pound note and decided to give it to whoever tells the biggest lie."

"You should be ashamed of yourselves," said the teacher, "When I was your age I didn't even know what a lie was."

The boys gave the ten pound note to the teacher.

A man walked up to the foreman of a road laying gang in Dingle and asked for a job. "I haven't got one for you today." said the foreman looking up from his newspaper. "But if you walk half a mile down here, you can see if you like the work and I can put you on the list for tomorrow." "That's great mate," said the bloke as he wandered off down the road to find the gang. At the end of the shift, the man walked past the foreman and shouted, "Thanks mate. See you tomorrow." The foreman looked up from his paper and shouted back, "You've enjoyed yourself then?". "Yes I have!" shouted back the bloke, "But can I have a shovel or a pick to lean on like the rest of the gang?"

Sam worked in an office in Allerton. One day he walked into his boss's office and said, "I'll be honest with you, I know the economy isn't great, but I have three companies after me, and I would like to respectfully ask for a pay rise."

After a few minutes of haggling, his manager finally agreed to a 5% rise, and Sam happily got up to leave.

"By the way", asked the boss as Sam got up, "Which three companies are after you?"

"The electric company, the water company and the phone company", Sam replied.

A man from Litherland wanted to become a monk so he went to the monastery and talked to the head monk. The head monk said, "You must take a vow of silence and can only say two words every three years."

The man agreed and after the first three years, the head monk came to him and said, "What are your two words?"

"Food cold!" the man replied.

Three more years went by and the head monk came to him and said "What are your two words?"

"Robe dirty!" the man exclaimed.

Three more years went by and the head monk came to him and said, "What are your two words?"

"I quit!" said the man.

"Well", the head monk replied, "I'm not surprised. You've done nothing but complain ever since you got here!"

England doesn't have a kidney bank, but it does have a Liverpool.

What is the difference between a battery and a Manchester United fan?

A battery has a positive side.

A lawyer from Manchester and a businessman from Formby from ended up sitting next to each other on a flight to airport.

The lawyer started thinking that he could have some fun at the Merseyside man's expense and asked him if he'd like to play a fun game. The Formby man was tired and just wanted to relax. He politely declined the offer and tried to sleep. The lawyer persisted, explaining:

"I ask you a question, and if you don't know the answer, you pay me only £5; you ask me one, and if I don't know the answer, I will pay you £500."

This got the Merseyside man a little more interested and he finally agreed to play the game.

The lawyer asked the first question, "What's the distance from the Earth to the moon?"

The businessman said nothing, but reached into his pocket, pulled out a five-pound note and handed it to the lawyer.

Now, it was the businessman's turn. He asked the lawyer, "What goes up a hill with three legs, and comes down with four?"

The lawyer used his laptop. He used the air-phone; he searched the web, he sent emails to his most well read friends, but still came up with nothing. After over an hour of searching, he finally gave up.

He woke up the businessman and handed him £500. The man smugly pocketed the cash and went straight back to sleep

The lawyer went wild with curiosity wanting to know the answer. He woke the businessman up and asked, "Well? What goes up a hill with three legs and comes down with four?"

The businessman reached into his pocket, handed the lawyer £5 and went back to sleep.

A visitor from outside the area was driving around Egremont in his fancy new car and realised that he was lost. The driver stopped old Tom and said, "You there! Old man, what happens if I turn left here?" "Don't know sir," replied Tom.

"Well what if I turn right here, where will that take me?" continued the visitor. "Don't know sir." replied old Tom. Becoming exasperated, the driver continued, "Well, what if I go straight on?" A flicker of knowledge moved over old Tom's face until he replied, "Don't know, sir." "I say old man you don't know a lot do you?" retorted the posh bloke. Old Tom looked at him and said, "I may not know a lot but I ain't lost like you are!" With that, old Tom walked off leaving the motorist stranded.

Robert proudly drove his new convertible into town and parked it on the main street he was on his way to the recycling centre to get rid of an unwanted gift, a footspa, which he left on the back seat.

He had walked half way down the street when he realised that he had left the top down... with the footspa in the back.

He ran all the way back to his car, but it was too late...

Another five footspas had been dumped in the car.

A passenger in a taxi travelling through Wallasey tapped the driver on the shoulder to ask him something. The driver screamed, lost control of the cab, nearly hit a bus, drove up over the curb and stopped just inches from a large plate glass window.

For a few moments everything was silent in the cab, then the driver said, "Please, don't ever do that again. You scared the daylights out of me."

The passenger, who was also frightened, apologised and said he didn't realise that a tap on the shoulder could frighten him so much, to which the driver replied, "I'm sorry, it's really not your fault at all. Today is my first day driving a cab. I've been driving a hearse for the last 25 years."

A man was rushing to a hospital from a business trip because his wife had just gone into labour with twins, and there was a strange family tradition that the first family member to arrive got to name the children. The man was afraid that his wayward brother would show up first and give his kids awful names. When he finally arrived at the hospital in a cold sweat he saw his brother sitting in the waiting room, waving, with a silly grin on his face. He walked unhappily in to see his wife who was scowling and holding two little babies, a boy and a girl. Almost afraid to hear it, the man asked, "What did he name the girl?" "Denise" says the wife. "Hey that's not too bad! What did he name the boy?" "De-nephew."

A man from Eastham phoned his son in London three days before Christmas and said, "I hate to ruin your day but I have to tell you that your mother and I are divorcing; forty-five years of misery is enough."

"Dad, what are you talking about?" his son shouted.

"We can't stand the sight of each other any longer" his father said, "We're sick of each other and I'm sick of talking about this, so you call your sister in Manchester and tell her."

Frantic, the son called his sister, who yelled "Like heck they're getting divorced!" she shouted, "I'll take care of this!"

She immediately called her father and yelled at him "You are not getting divorced. Don't do a single thing until I get there. I'm calling my brother back, and we'll both be there tomorrow. Until then, don't do a thing, DO YOU HEAR ME?". Then she hung up.

The old man hung up his phone and turned to his wife. "Sorted! They're coming for Christmas - and they're paying their own way."

A Hunt's Cross man fell out with his in-laws and banned them from entering the house while he was in it. His wife faithfully carried out his wishes until she was on her death bed and then asked sadly, "Haven't I always been a supportive wife to you, John?" "Yes my dear." He replied "The best".

"Then I would love it if you could grant my last request and let my sister Sarah ride in the first car with you at my funeral?"

"Alright, my dear" he agreed heavily, "But I'm warning you, it'll spoil all my pleasure!"

Jim was having a pint in Ma Egerton's one night when in walked Simon, a very brash man from Manchester. Jim couldn't help overhearing Simon trying to encourage some people to bet that they couldn't drink 20 pints in 20 minutes. Despite a great deal of persuasion, Simon was still failing in his attempt to make some money. Then he looked at Jim and said "Well what about you then? Are you interested?" Jim quickly drank the rest of his pint and left the pub.

Half an hour later, Jim walked back into the pub and said to Simon "OK, I'll take that bet."

Simon was delighted at the thought of winning the bet. But his excitement soon faded when Jim drank down the 20 pints in 19 minutes. Handing over the money, Simon said "When you left here earlier, where did you go?" Jim looked at him and replied "I had to go to pub down the road to see if I could do it first."

Four Liverpool University students taking their chemistry degree had done very well in their exams so far.

Because of this, even though their last exam of the year was fast approaching, the four friends decided to go back to their home town and catch up with some friends there.

They had a great time. However, after all the fun, they slept all day on Sunday and didn't make it back to town until early Monday morning which was the morning of their final exam.

Rather than taking the exam, they decided to find their professor after it was over and explain to him why they missed it.

They told him that they had gone home to do some studying for the weekend with the plan to come back in time for the exam.

But unfortunately, they had a flat tyre on the way back, didn't have a spare, and couldn't get help for a long time. As a result, they had only just arrived!

The professor thought it over and then agreed they could make up their final exam the following day.

The four were very relieved. They studied hard that night - all night - and went in the next day at the time the professor had told them.

He placed them in separate rooms and handed each of them a test booklet and told them to begin. The first problem was worth five points. It was something simple about a specific chemistry topic.

"Great," they all thought, "This is going to be easy."

They each finished the problem and turned the page.

On the second page was written, 'Question 2 (for 95 points): Which tyre?

A man was hitchhiking back to Moreton at night when he was caught in the middle of a big storm.

It was growing darker and no cars seemed to be coming by. The rain was so heavy that the man could hardly see a few feet ahead of him

Suddenly, he saw a car slowly coming towards him and stopped. Desperate for shelter and without thinking about it, he jumped into the car and closed the door. But then he realised there was nobody behind the wheel and the engine wasn't on.

The car started moving slowly. The man looked out and saw that the car was approaching a bend in the road. Terrified, he started to pray, begging for his life. Suddenly, just before the car hit the verge, a disembodied hand seemed to appear from nowhere through the car window and turn the wheel. The man stared in horror at the hand, though it didn't come near him.

Soon after, the man noticed the lights of a pub appear down the road. He found the strength to leap out of the car and ran towards it. Wet and out of breath, he rushed inside and started telling everybody about the horrible experience he had just had.

A silence fell on the people in the pub when they realised how scared the student was.

Suddenly, the door opened, and two other people walked in.

Like the Moreton man, they were also soaked and out of breath. Looking around, and seeing the man standing shaking at the bar, one said to the other..

"Look mate...there's the idiot that got in the car while we were pushing it!"

A well known Philosophy professor from Liverpool University was giving a lecture on the philosophy of language and came to a curious aspect of the English language.

"You will note," said the somewhat stuffy scholar, "That in the English language, two negatives can mean a positive, but it is never the case that two positives can mean a negative."

To which someone at the back responded, "Yeah, yeah."

A father and his son, Bobby, arrived at the big match at Anfield and Dad suddenly realised that he couldn't find their tickets.

He said to his son, "Nip home and see if I left the tickets there."

Bobby replied "No probs, Dad." Half an hour later Bobby returned to his dad who was patiently waiting outside the football pitch.

He said to his dad, "Yep, they're on the kitchen table where you left them."

A Mancunian was once walking through the desert when he stumbled across an old lamp. He picked it up and rubbed it and a genie appeared before his eyes.

"You have two wishes," said the genie "Use them wisely."

So he said "I want an everlasting pie!"

The genie gave him a pie. He wolfed half of it and said "Mmm that's good.

"I'll have another of these."

A teacher at a Liverpool School was having a little trouble getting her year 11 pupils to understand grammar, "These are what we call the pronouns", she explained, "And the way we use them with verbs; I am, you are, he/she is" she was added, to blank looks.

Trying a different approach, she said, "Susan, give me a sentence with the pronoun, 'I' in it."

Susan began, "I is..."

"No, no, no, no, no NO, NO!", shouted the teacher, "Never, 'I is', always, 'I am'... now try again".

Susan looked puzzled and a little hurt, thought a while then began again more quietly, "I... am...the ninth letter of the alphabet".

A vicar from New Ferry was travelling home one evening and was greatly annoyed when a young man, much the worse for drink, came and sat next to him on the bus.

"Young man," the vicar, declared in a rather pompous tone, "Do you not realise you are on the road to perdition?"

"Oh, drat and botheration," replied the drunken man, "I could have sworn this bus went to Lunt."

At a pub in Crosby, a newcomer asked a local "Have you lived here all your life?"

After a long pause the man replied "Don't know yet!"

At a well established manufacturing business in Birkenhead, the young boss had the sad responsibility of telling one of the workers, Joe, that it was time for him to retire after 60 years with the company.

The old man was outraged:

"So, it's come to this, has it? I'm not wanted any longer?" he protested.

"I worked for your father, your grandfather and his dad too.

I tell you what, young man, if I'd known that this job wasn't going to be permanent, I would never have taken it on."

A boy from Seacombe was getting ready to start his new school term. Because he was getting older and more independent, his father gave him £2 for him to catch the bus home. But instead of getting on the bus, the boy ran behind it all the way home. His father came home and the boy proudly said, "Dad, I saved you £2 today because I ran behind the bus instead of getting on!" The man stormed out of the room, shouting "You should have run behind a taxi and saved me 40 quid you little..."

How many Chelsea fans does it take to change a light bulb?

None, they're all happy living in Liverpool shadow!

A man was sitting in a cafe in Bromborough, he was fed up and had come out for a bit of company and to try and cheer him-self up. He picked up the menu and noticed that it only featured three dishes: meatloaf, shepherd's pie and Yorkshire pudding. The waitress came over to take his order. "I'll have the Yorkshire pudding," said the man glumly, "and if you could throw in a few kind words that would be very welcome." The waitress left and returned a few minutes later with a plate of Yorkshire pudding. She banged the plate on the table in front of the man and started to walk off. "Hey," said the man. "I got my dinner; how about those kind words?" The waitress turned, paused and said, "Don't eat the Yorkshire pudding."

Jim, a Dovecot man, found himself in dire trouble. He had already lost his business and was experiencing further financial problems. He decided to ask God for help. "God, please help me. I've lost my business and if I don't get my hands on some money, I'm going to lose my house too. Please let me win the lottery!"

Lottery night came and went but Jim didn't win. So he prayed again. "God, please let me win the lottery! I've lost my business, my house and I'm going to lose my car as well!"

Lottery night came and went again! Still no luck... Jim prayed again

"I've lost my business, my house and my car. I don't often ask you for help. PLEASE just let me win the lottery this one time so I can get back on my feet!"

Suddenly there is a blinding flash as the heavens open and the voice of God Himself thunders:

"Jim at least meet Me half way and buy a ticket!"

A man from Woolton was building a garden shed and he ran out of nails so he went to the hardware store to buy some more. "How long do you want them?" asked the assistant. "Oh, I need to keep them." replied the man.

A Mancunian was going for a job interview in Liverpool city centre and on the way there, he asked a local man for directions:

"Excuse me mate could you possibly tell me the quickest way to Liverpool city centre?"

The man replied: "You driving or walking, lad?"

The Mancunian replied: "Driving."

The Liverpool man nodded, saying:

"Yup, definitely the quickest way"

When Steve moved to London he constantly annoyed his new acquaintances by boasting about how great his home town of Liverpool was.

Finally, in exasperation, one said, "If Liverpool is so wonderful, how come you didn't stay there?" "Well," answered Steve "They're all so clever up there I had to come down here to have any chance of making it at all."

Andy and Martin were delighted that they had finished a jigsaw puzzle in record time and told Louise that the hundred pieces had only taken them six months to fit together. Their friend, Louise was unimpressed and said that it sounded like a long time to complete a jigsaw puzzle. "Not at all" replied Andy, "It said on the box three to five years."

A dog ran into a butcher's shop in West Derby and grabbed some sirloin steak off the counter. But the butcher recognized the dog as belonging to a neighbour of his who happened to be a lawyer. The butcher called up his neighbour and said, "If your dog stole steak from my butcher shop, would you be liable for the cost of the meat?" The lawyer replied, "Of course, how much was the sirloin?" The butcher replied "Seven pounds." A few days later the butcher received a cheque for seven pounds - and an invoice stating "Legal Consultation Service: £150."

A Mancunian went into a hardware store and asked to buy a sink.

"Would you like one with a plug?" asked the assistant. "Don't tell me they've gone electric!" said the man.

A high-rise building was going up in Liverpool's commercial district, and three steel erectors sat on a girder having their lunch. "Oh, no, not cream cheese and cucumber again", said the first, who came from Islington. "If I get the same again tomorrow, I'll jump off the girder."

The second, who came from Ropewalks, opened his packet. "Oh, no, not salami and lettuce on wholegrain again," he said. "If I get the same again tomorrow, I'll jump off too."

The third man, who came from Canning, opened his lunch. "Oh, no, not another cheese sandwich," he said. "If I get the same again tomorrow, I'll follow you two off the girder."

The next day, the Islington man got cream cheese and cucumber. Without delay, he jumped. The Ropewalks man saw

he had salami and lettuce on wholegrain. With a wild cry, he leapt too. The Canning man then opened his lunchbox. "Oh, no," he said. "Cheese sandwiches." And he too jumped. The foreman, who had overheard their conversation, reported what had happened, and the funerals were held together.

"If only I'd known," sobbed the wife of the Islington man. "If only he'd said," cried the wife of the Ropewalks man. "I don't understand it at all," said the wife of the Canning man. "He always got his own sandwiches ready."

A priest was visiting Liverpool and while taking a trip to the seaside he looked out to sea where two Liverpool supporters were out in a boat. Suddenly he noticed that in the water, an Everton fan was being attacked by a shark. Fortunately, a boat arrived and the Liverpool fans pulled the Man City fan into the boat to safety, killed the shark and pulled it onto the boat.

The priest beckoned the boat to the shore and said "I've never seen anything so brave. I understood that there was intense rivalry between Liverpool and Man City fans but that has restored my faith in mankind". He then blessed the men and left.

One of the locals turned to his friend and asked "What was he on about?"

"Dunno" said his mate "But he knows nothing all about shark fishing. Do we need any fresh bait?"

At an antiques auction in Liverpool, a wealthy American announced that he had lost his wallet containing £5,000, and he would give a reward of £50 to the person who found it. From the back of the hall a local man shouted, "I'll give £100!"

Why were Chelsea late for their next big match? They were stuck on a broken escalator!

A couple from Tranmere had been courting for nearly twenty years. One day as they sat on a seat in the park, the woman plucked up the courage to ask,

"Don't you think it's time we got married?"

Her sweetheart answered,

"Yes, but who'd have us?"

A labourer shouted up to his roofer mate on top of an old terraced house in Greasby, saying, "Don't start climbing down this ladder, Burt." "Why not?" Burt called back. "Cos I moved it five minutes ago!" replied his mate.

One day a man walked into a bar in Liverpool and ordered a beer. He took his first sip and put it down. While he was looking around the bar, a monkey leapt down and stole the pint of beer so swiftly that there was nothing he could do. The man asked who owned the thieving little monkey and the barman pointed to the bloke playing the piano. The man walked over and says "Oi - do you know your monkey just stole my blooming beer?" The pianist replied "No, but if you hum it, I'll play it."

They say that a man from Manchester laughs three times at a joke: the first time when everybody gets it, the second a week later when he thinks he gets it, the third time a month later when somebody explains it to him.

Unusual place and street names

Lickers Lane

Menlove Avenue, Liverpool

Ogle Close, Prescot

Slag Lane, Haydock

Tickle Avenue, St Helens

How many Mancunians does it take to change a light bulb?
Two - one to change the bulb, the other to say loudly how he
did it as well as anyone from Liverpool.

At a cricket match at Aigburth, a fast bowler sent one down and it just clipped the bail.

As nobody yelled "Ow's at!" the batsman picked up the bail and replaced it.

He looked at the umpire and said "Windy today isn't it?"

"Yes," said the umpire "It is. Make sure it doesn't blow your cap off when you walk back to the pavilion."